T0194999

Fingerprints
of God

A 30 Day Devotional and Journal

RUTH SMITH

WESTBOW
PRESS®
A DIVISION OF THOMAS NELSON
& ZONDERVAN

WestBow Press books may be ordered through booksellers or by contacting:

WestBow Press
A Division of Thomas Nelson & Zondervan
1663 Liberty Drive
Bloomington, IN 47403
www.westbowpress.com
844-714-3454

Because of the dynamic nature of the Internet, any web addresses or links contained in this book may have changed since publication and may no longer be valid. The views expressed in this work are solely those of the author and do not necessarily reflect the views of the publisher, and the publisher hereby disclaims any responsibility for them.

Any people depicted in stock imagery provided by Getty Images are models, and such images are being used for illustrative purposes only.
Certain stock imagery © Getty Images.

Bannie McCormick as the digital cover designer

Scripture marked (NKJV) taken from the New King James Version®. Copyright © 1982 by Thomas Nelson. Used by permission. All rights reserved.

Scripture quotations marked (NIV) are taken from the Holy Bible, New International Version®, NIV®. Copyright © 1973, 1978, 1984, 2011 by Biblica, Inc.® Used by permission of Zondervan. All rights reserved worldwide. www.zondervan.com The "NIV" and "New International Version" are trademarks registered in the United States Patent and Trademark Office by Biblica, Inc.®

ISBN: 978-1-6642-8694-8 (sc)
ISBN: 978-1-6642-8695-5 (hc)
ISBN: 978-1-6642-8693-1 (e)

Print information available on the last page.

WestBow Press rev. date: 4/10/2023

CONTENTS

CREDITS

I want to thank God for the way He has worked through my life and in the months leading up to writing this devotional. I am not an author; I am a tool. The author is my Heavenly Father and I pray that He will use me through this devotional to impact the lives of many. We are all on a journey which will lead us somewhere. My prayer is that my journey will lead others to the Author.

I also want to thank Jennifer, Julie, and Debbie for always being my support and sisters in Christ. You have always been willing and ready to help me grow deeper in my faith and there are no three other women I would have rather been on this journey with. Thank you for being the best godly friends I could have ever asked or prayed for.

Thank you to my husband, Jim, who was willing to trust the decision that God was leading me to, and for standing with me as I stepped out on faith and loving me unconditionally. Your love and support are the reasons it has been an easy transition. I love you and the way you love me.

I am blessed to have each of you in my life.
In memory of my dad and son-in-law

INTRODUCTION

As Christians, we long to see, hear, and feel God in our lives. In reality, however, we have to stop, look, and listen. How many of us can look back and see where God has been in our lives? We seek and search and we long to hear from Him, but too often we fail to see the fingerprints He has left behind.

As I have longed to hear God speak in my own life, I have learned that He is always speaking. I just have to be on His channel to hear Him. Get in the will of God to block out the static so that you are in tune with Him.

We can let Satan rule, or we can let our Lord have supreme control in our lives. Have faith, my friends, and allow Christ to be Lord of your lives, experience the Spirit's power, and see the fingerprints He has left in your own lives. My prayer for you as you read and journal the next thirty days would be for you to hear God speak, feel His presence, and see His fingerprints.

> Trust in the Lord and do good, dwell in the land, and feed on His faithfulness. Delight yourself also in the Lord, and He shall give you the desires of your heart. Commit your way to the Lord, trust also in Him, and He shall bring it to pass. (Psalm 37:3–5 NKJV)

DAY 1

The Lesson of the Sourdough Bread

Sometimes we ask the Lord to answer prayers in specific ways. I am learning that His ways are not my ways. For two years, I have prayed for God to give me the desire of my heart: to be able to stay home and take care of my parents and eventually my husband while working as an independent beauty consultant full time. I have asked God as Gideon to take my forty-hour-a-week job away from me, if that was what He wanted me to do. As I learn that His ways are not my ways, I am also learning that He is asking me to step out on faith and to trust Him. I am learning to listen to Him speak and responding to His request. Is it hard? Absolutely. Will it be worth it? Absolutely. He has spoken to me in many ways over the last few weeks, even being comical and making me laugh. The lesson of the sourdough bread has been the loudest.

As I visited the Amish store in search of canning salt, I found myself drawn to the sourdough bread. Let's face it. You can't go to the Amish store without buying sourdough bread. As I have battled hearing God speak to me, I am also learning to trust in His provision. The morning after I purchased the sourdough bread, I woke up in anticipation of how good it would be. I proceeded to cut off two one-inch-thick slices and loaded on the butter as I heated the iron skillet with my mouth watering. As I fixed my toast, a dear friend sent me her "daily bread" devotional. Knowing my situation, she felt led to share it with me. What I had been struggling with was brought to life in those words.

Reading the devotional as my bread toasted, God spoke loudly and clearly as He proceeded to let me know that He would provide for me and my family. It may not be fancy sourdough bread with twice the price of the bread I usually purchased, but it would be sufficient. The toast was a little hard to swallow that morning, but I got the message. The following morning, I got up and cut off two slices of the sourdough bread, about a third of the size from the previous morning. He doesn't want us to waste what He has provided, even during a lesson, right? As I buttered the bread that morning with more than enough butter, He spoke once again: "Do you need that much butter, or will a little be sufficient?" "Okay, Lord," I said as I scraped off the excess butter with a smile on my face, "it is sufficient."

By the third morning, I didn't even get the bread out of the bag, and He was at it again. As I looked at the sourdough bread, He let me know that the bread I had been eating was enough with a little bit of butter. Every morning, I put honey—a good amount of honey, I might add—on my toast, and this morning would start out no differently. As I turned the jar of honey upside down with a hefty squeeze, He spoke once again. "Do you need to smother it with honey, or will a little be sufficient?" With a chuckle and the thought *Really, God?* I set the honey down and began to lightly coat my toast with a butter knife and a little bit of honey.

By the fourth morning, I got it. *My simple bread, easy on the butter, and a light coat of honey*—or so I thought. As I pulled my two slices of bread out of the bag, God said, "Do you need two slices, or will one be sufficient?" By this time, I was full-blown laughing. *One will do.*

God can speak to us in unusual ways sometimes. We just have to be willing to listen. I know that God will provide as I transition into my full-time career as an independent beauty consultant. He just asked that I trust Him.

What lesson is God trying to teach you?

_____

_____

_____

_____

_____

_____

_____

_____

_____

_____

_____

_____

_____

_____

_____

_____

_____

_____

_____

_____

_____

_____

_____

_____

"For My thoughts are not your thoughts, nor are your ways My ways," says the Lord. "For as the heavens are higher than the earth, so are My ways higher than your ways, and My thoughts than your thoughts." (Isaiah 55:8–9 NKJV)

DAY 2

The Whys in Life

Have you ever wondered why God allows thing to happen? As I see His fingerprints on my life more and more, I see the times I was out of the will of God. In 2006, my husband and I were in the process of building our home. Our plan was to house missionaries while they worked in and around our town. Our two daughters had joined a group of youth in missions a few years earlier, and I just knew this was what we were meant to do.

When we broke ground, we had a circle of prayer right where the house would sit. We would work late hours into the night, but we always stopped by midnight on Saturday evenings to not work on the Lord's Sabbath. This house was to be used for Him, and we did not want to defile it with disobedience.

We had been working on the house for over a year, doing some of the work ourselves to save money. However, it ended up costing us a lot of blood, sweat, tears, and time. There were so many mishaps and close calls that we were able to thank God for the ways they ended. Perhaps the most eye-opening was the event that happened on June 5, 2006. We were working hard to complete some things because a group of missionaries from Florida were arriving that day to see the progress on the house.

As we worked on the fireplace in an open-to-below living room, my husband fell twenty-one feet and hit his face on a framed hearth made of two-inch by eight-inch boards. He ended up with seven fractures in his face, which was deeply cut from the inside corner of his right eye down below his cheek and back up toward his ear.

There were many emotions that day, but we knew God had His

hand on him. My husband's thoughts were that he wasn't living his life right. My thoughts were more focused on God not being done with him yet as He reached out His hand to catch him from a fall that could have been fatal.

From a twenty-one-foot fall to a pile of pine railing sliding off the second floor and hitting right where my family had just been sitting, shattering the bathroom vanity top to struggling to make house payments over the years, God has been there to pick us up. We have been in our home for almost sixteen years now, but it has only been in the last year or so that I have realized we were out of the will of God. We never asked God to reveal His plans to us. Should we have built this house? Was it what God wanted us to do? I think sometimes God allows things to happen to bring us back and have us cry out to Him.

Our life has gotten much easier over the last few years. That doesn't mean it has been a piece of cake though. Was it that our luck had finally turned around? I think not. We are seeking God and His will for our lives, and we are learning that God has to let us go through storms to get our attention. He got our attention through some difficult times, but only now am I seeing His fingerprints. Consider this: instead of asking God, "Why is this happening to me?" try asking Him, "What, God, is Your will for my life?" God will use discipline and reminders to bring us back into His will, but it will be easier to seek His will first.

What is God's will for your life?

Unless the Lord builds the house, they labor in vain who built it, unless the Lord guards the city, the watchman stays awake in vain. (Psalm 127:1 NKJV)

The Lord is my Shepherd; I shall not want.
He makes me to lie down in green pastures;
He leads me beside the still waters.
He restores my soul;
He leads me in the paths of righteousness
For His name's sake.
Yea, though I walk through the valley of the shadow of death,
I will fear no evil;
For You are with me;
Your rod and Your staff, they comfort me.
You prepare a table before me in the presence of my enemies;
You anoint my head with oil;
My cup runs over.
Surely goodness and mercy shall follow me
All the days of my life;
And I will dwell in the house of the Lord forever. (Psalm 23 NKJV)

RUTH SMITH

DAY 3

Facing Jericho

My pastor preached about Joshua and what he faced at Jericho: a wall that was big and so mighty. How could he ever defeat his Jericho? As the pastor preached, I thought of all the Jerichos in my life right now. I know everyone's Jericho is different. Sometimes one's Jericho can seem petty compared to others, especially when someone is fighting cancer or other life-threatening illnesses or the loss of a child or other loved ones. My financial burdens and stress are no comparison to that, but it is a Jericho to me.

I actually made a list of my family's Jerichos, and you may want to do the same. It allowed me to ask for guidance and help to defeat each one of my Jerichos by calling each one out. You may only have one Jericho right now, or you may be like my family and have nine. No matter how many you are facing, there is a big, mighty God who is there to help you face them and to break down that wall to get you to other side. I challenge you to march around your kitchen table as you pray about the walls that need to come down. Ask God to help you fight the battle and He will show you the fingerprints of where He has been during it all.

What's your Jericho?

_____
_____
_____
_____
_____
_____
_____
_____
_____
_____
_____
_____
_____
_____
_____
_____
_____
_____
_____
_____
_____
_____
_____
_____
_____
_____

And the Lord said to Joshua: "See! I have given Jericho into your hand, its king, and the mighty men of valor." (Joshua 6:2 NKJV)

DAY 4

Reaching for the Unseen

It is easy for most of us to see something, reach out, and get it. We reach for a glass when we need a drink, a piece of dirt lying on the floor, and even a particle floating in the air like a dandelion cast by a breeze. Now consider what you can't see, like the wind or even the physical body of Christ.

My dad struggles with dementia, and it is hard to watch him decline. Most days he will laugh and talk with us; other days he will repeat himself, be a bit confused, or just sit quietly. On his worst days, he will reach for the unseen—unseen by us, that is. Hallucinations paint vivid pictures in his mind, so to him they exist. Whether he is seeing a family member from the past, reaching at shadows on the floor, or seeing animals under the bed, the unseen is very real to him.

We can't see what a person with dementia sees, but to that person it is there. Even though we didn't have the chance to physically walk and talk with Jesus, as Christians we can do the same as someone with dementia: we too, have a vivid picture in our mind and heart of Christ. While we can't physically see Him, we see His manifest presence, and the fingerprints that are left behind.

It is hard to show someone who is an unbeliever what we see. While that person can't see Him, we can start revealing Him to that person by letting Jesus live in us. There will always be someone reaching for the unseen. God can use us to paint a picture so that it is as vivid and reachable to those who seek as to someone who has already seen. They will want what they can't see (Jesus) too.

Are you reaching for the unseen?

_____

_____

_____

_____

_____

_____

_____

_____

_____

_____

_____

_____

_____

_____

_____

_____

_____

_____

_____

_____

_____

_____

While we do not look at the things which are seen, but at the things which are not seen. For the things which are seen are temporary, but the things which are not seen are eternal. (2 Corinthians 4:18 NKJV)

RUTH SMITH

DAY 5

Fear Not

I think fear is the one thing that we all have in common, but why? "Fear not" is used in the Bible 365 times, yet it is one thing that we allow to take control over us. You may be sitting there reading this and thinking *I'm not scared of anything*, but we all have fears. Whether it is a fear of spiders, storms, water, heights, or even death, we all have something. How we handle that fear is something entirely different. Isaiah 41:10 (NKJV) reminds us to "Fear not, for I am with you, be not dismayed, for I am your God."

As a young teenager and tomboy, I remember one fall when my dad and oldest brother had been out cutting wood. I can remember the yelling and the sight of my brother sitting in the kitchen chair with his knee bleeding and the torn flesh through his jeans. He had been cutting a limb and as the limb kicked back, it caused the chainsaw to kick back also, catching my brother's knee. For many years, I have had a fear of chainsaws. I didn't want to be around them while they were running, let alone run one. I didn't know then, but God was using that accident to show me His fingerprint later in my life. If the accident had not happened, I would not have had the fear of chainsaws for God to remove.

Only a few years ago, when a neighbor had given my husband and me about seventeen loads of logs to cut up for firewood, did I start to let that fear go. My husband had just been through his fourth back surgery about four months before God blessed us with the wood. The logs had already been trimmed, so all we had to do was to load, unload, cut into blocks, and split the wood to fit into our fireplace. My husband was already doing more with the wood than he should have been because of his back. It was time for me to suck it up buttercup, get the chainsaw in hand, and go to work. I was terrified to say the least for the first hour or two. I had to put my eyes and focus on Jesus instead of the circumstances. Does it mean that I have no more fears? Of course not.

I have a fear that looms over me, or should I say under me. I still fight the fear of heights. That's a hard one for me to let go of, but with prayer and focusing on the Lord I have started to let go of that one some as well. I have been able to travel a little over the last four or five years. I never thought I would ever get on a plane because of my fear of heights. However, by putting my eyes on Him, I actually enjoy flying. With that said, I still have no intentions of going sky diving, getting in a hot air balloon, or standing on the edge of a cliff. If I was forced to do those things, I know where my eyes would be. Jesus triumphs over circumstance and faith over fear.

What fear has its hold on you?

_____
_____
_____
_____
_____
_____
_____
_____
_____
_____
_____
_____
_____
_____
_____
_____
_____
_____
_____
_____
_____
_____

I sought the Lord, and He heard me, and delivered me
from all my fears. (Psalm 34:4 NKJV)

DAY 6

Supernatural Strength

It was a cool overcast fall day in 1983. My dad was running a 160-acre farm for a convent of nuns. There was always work to be done, and silage chopping season was in full swing. If you're unsure of what that is, here's a little description. Farmers like my dad would grow corn and, in the fall, they used a piece of equipment that would chop up the corn and blow it into a silage wagon. They would take the load of silage (chopped up corn stalks) to the barn and connect it to a machine that would blow it up several lengths of pipes into the silo. It would be housed there until time to use it for feed during the winter.

My dad and brother had brought the first load of silage to the barn that morning. As my dad started unloading the silage, he sent my brother to the barn to get some burnt oil. They would put this on the chains that brought the silage from the back of the wagon to the front where there were three beaters the width of the wagon and full of three-inch teeth. Think about giant rolling pins with metal spikes all turning in different directions to move the silage out of the wagon. The wagon was almost empty other than some at the back and sides of the wagon that hadn't traveled down the conveyor chains. As Dad had done so many times before, he threw a pitchfork into the wagon so he could climb in and move the rest of the silage onto the chains to empty the wagon. This time, the beaters caught his jacket and started pulling him between them. My dad said he remembered getting pulled in as he fought to stop it. God was truly in control. He remembers yelling for help and the Lord heard his cry.

As my brother was coming back from the barn, he heard what sounded like a cow balling only to find our dad fighting against the wagon that was trying to pull him in. My brother was able to turn off the tractor and disengage the operation of the wagon. Dad came out of what could have been a tragic accident with only a scratch on his back through his heavy coat and a plug out of the side of his nose the size of a pencil eraser that was reattached with only three stitches. The most amazing part of the story is the reminder and fingerprint of God that we have still to this day: a quarter-inch thick metal cog that was bent and broken from the supernatural strength the Lord gave him that day. I am reminded of the verse in Philippians 4:13 (NKJV): "I can do all things through Christ who strengthens me." I am thankful for the strength God gave my dad that day and I am thankful for the fingerprint He left for us to see.

What do you need to ask God supernatural strength for?

May the Lord answer you in the day of trouble. (Psalm 20:1 NKJV)

DAY 7

FOG

A mountain is an elevated portion of the earth, generally with steep sides that will lead to its highest point. A hill is easier to climb than a mountain because it is less steep and not as high, but like a mountain a hill leads you to its highest point. A valley, on the other hand, is a low area of land between hills or mountains, a low point, or a path between the mountains.

Not long after I had started writing this devotional, my best friend told me a story about her morning drive to work. On that drive, she would come to a place between a mountain and a valley. Sometimes it would be filled with fog that she couldn't see through. She knew there was something about it that God was trying to reveal to her. She took a picture of it one morning but never shared it with anyone. Then one morning on her way to work, the fog broke and God revealed to her that sometimes we must look through and past the fog to see what God has in store for us. As the fog broke, she found herself between a beautiful mountain and a lush green valley with a river running through it and the sun peeking through. She had questioned what the fog represented. It wasn't until after I had revealed the title of this devotional, *Fingerprints of God*, to her that she understood. Sometimes the FOG must be lifted and God will use the beauty and wonders of nature to speak to us.

We will all journey through the hills and valleys with highs and lows in our lives. We don't get to the tops of the mountains on our own and we do not go through the valleys alone. He is in the midst of it all whether we see the mountains as obstacles or as places where everything is good. Being in valleys may be our lowest points or pathways around obstacles. Don't fail to see the FOG as His beauty is revealed.

Is the FOG obstructing your view or do you see the fingerprints of God?

I will lift up my eyes to the hills-whence comes my help?
My help comes from the Lord, who made heaven and
earth. (Psalm 121:1–2 NKJV)

DAY 8

You Little Looker

"You little looker" has become a common phrase in our home when we play Shanghai rummy. The more people who play, the more difficult the game and the closer we sit to each other. The object of the game is to have the lowest score by laying down your cards first when you complete each round. Then the other players can look at what you have laid down and play on them.

One night while playing, someone was trying to see what the other person was playing and out came "You little looker." As silly as it is and the way it makes us laugh each time someone says it makes that phrase relevant in our daily lives as well.

We are all looking for something or at someone. Those who are looking in are trying to find meaning in life, ever seeking after the world rather than the truth: God. Those who are looking back see where they could have done something different and maybe made their lives better. Those looking around in search of the happiness they see in others, wondering, *What do they have?* Then there are those who are looking forward and eventually up because there is nowhere else to look. Only then are we able to fix our eyes on the things above. After all the temporary fixes, we can finally see that Jesus is the only fix we need. This doesn't mean that we will never be little lookers again. We will always need to search for something; there will always be little lookers watching us to see if we mess up or to want what they see we have. Someone is always watching, and we will always be witnesses, good or bad, in everything we do and say. You are the cards, so what do you want the lookers to see? Help others to see the fingerprints of God in your life, that one day they may hold the winning hand of Jesus.

What do others see when they look at you?

_____
_____
_____
_____
_____
_____
_____
_____
_____
_____
_____
_____
_____
_____
_____
_____
_____
_____
_____
_____
_____
_____

"Look to Me, and be saved, all you ends of the earth! For I am God, and there is no other." (Isaiah 45:22 NKJV)

DAY 9

Motivated By Rejection

For five years while I worked at a diagnostic center, I had the opportunity to pray with patients who had upcoming surgeries or hear things they felt comfortable sharing with me. It's funny how much you can learn from someone in such a short period of time.

It was a pre-op day where several patients would have labs, EKGs and x-rays done before attending a class where they would be informed about their upcoming procedures.

I had the opportunity to pray with several people that day. That was also the first and only time in that five years I was rejected as I asked if I could pray for a gentleman that I was taking care of. My heart hurt for him and for the young girl with him as he responded, "I don't think so." All I could do was to tell him that I would pray for him in my quiet time. At that point it wasn't even about his upcoming surgery; it was about his salvation.

As Christians, we can be rejected and persecuted for our faith, but it can't be taken away from us. Even if you are rejected, be motivated to pray even more fervently for that individual and his or her need for Christ. We are to intercede for those who are dying.

Even though I was not physically or verbally persecuted that day, it was a day that Satan would try to use my rejection as a way to mentally persecute me. He wants to use those times to attack us with fear and a feeling of defeat to try to prevent us from sharing or praying again. I am thankful God has given me a heart to pray for others, for even in times of rejection my heart is able to intercede for them.

How will you respond to rejection?

_____
_____
_____
_____
_____
_____
_____
_____
_____
_____
_____
_____
_____
_____
_____
_____
_____
_____
_____
_____
_____
_____

Therefore, I exhort first of all that supplications, prayers, intercessions, and giving of thanks be made for all men. (1 Timothy 2:1 NKJV)

DAY 10

You Are Not Alone

Have you ever been snipe hunting? A snipe hunt is a practical joke mainly played by young adults and teenagers on unsuspecting newcomers and kids. The object of the joke is to talk the young victim into trying to catch a bird called a snipe, which typically lives in wet marshy settings such as swamps. After dark, the newcomer is led out into a field or into the woods with a bag to catch the snipe. Everyone else supposedly chases the bird to the person so he or she can catch it. In reality, they are leaving the person all alone holding a bag that will never be filled.

If you have ever been outside at night, whether it is in your backyard or in the woods, it can be scary when you are alone. The more we think about the dark and being alone, the more unsettled we become. Loneliness itself can put us in a state of fear. In snipe hunting, we allow others to put us in the position of being alone. In the walk of life, at times we allow ourselves to be alone, whether by pushing someone away or distancing ourselves from him or her. The same can be said about Christians when we get out of the word of God, or when we allow our relationships and prayer lives be taken over by the busyness of this world. As Christians, we are never alone, because we have a friend in Jesus. He doesn't turn His back on us, but sometimes we turn our backs on Him. He will never leave us, although we may leave the comfort of Him. He waits patiently to hold us in His arms and pull us close to Him.

When you are feeling alone ask yourself, *Why do I feel alone?* Am I in God's word, am I talking to Him daily, am I allowing Him to walk along beside me? This world can be a lonely place, but He is there to comfort us, and we can rest assured that we are never alone when we have caught Jesus.

What makes you feel alone?

_____
_____
_____
_____
_____
_____
_____
_____
_____
_____
_____
_____
_____
_____
_____
_____
_____
_____
_____
_____
_____

For I will never leave you nor forsake you. (Hebrews 13:5 NKJV)

DAY 11

A Year of Adversity

The year of 2020 will go down in the books as one of the most trying times in history. So many have been sick, and so many have lost their lives. The destruction of COVID-19 has taken a toll on all of us. Through it all, COVID has revealed three types of people.

The first type is angry, full of hate, distrust, and bitterness. These feelings could have been expressed through rioting, violence, sinful attitudes toward the government and others, or being focused on the negative aspect of the circumstances. I can say that I do not always agree with the decisions that the government has made, but I do believe that we are to pray for those in government to make godly decisions. As 1 Timothy 2:1–4 (NKJV) states, "Therefore I exhort first of all that supplications, prayers, intercessions, and giving of thanks be made for all men, for Kings, and all who are in authority, that we may lead a quiet and peaceable life in all godliness and reverence. For this is good and acceptable in the sight of God our Savior, who desires all men to be saved an to come to the knowledge of the truth."

The second type of person is one I call a fence rider. They believe in the Lord, maybe love the Lord, and pray for the adversities to go away. However, they do not truly trust in the Lord to heal our land and see us through. Maybe they harbor resentment and allow others to influence their actions and decisions. Revelations 3:15–16 (NKJV) talks about being lukewarm. It states, "I know your works, that you are neither cold nor hot. I could wish you were cold or hot, so then because you are lukewarm, and neither cold nor hot, I will vomit you out of my mouth." I know we all become lukewarm at times, but God wants us to be on fire for Him, which leads me to the third type of person.

This is a person who seeks answers from the Lord, one who trusts Him to see us through, who is willing to focus on the positive, and who trusts that the Lord's will be done. This person cries out to the Lord to heal our land and to rescue the lost before it is too late. This person believes in unity and becoming stronger in his or her walk and faith. As Matthew 12:30 and 33 (NKJV) explains, "He who is not with Me is against Me, and he who does not gather with Me scatters abroad." We are to be His witnesses, and we are, whether for good or evil. Verse 33 states, "Either make the tree good and its fruit good or else make the tree bad and its fruit bad; for a tree is known by its fruit."

What have you displayed over the past years? Have you been on fire for the Lord and made known your good fruits, or have you born bad fruit for others to see? I pray others have seen the fingerprints of God in your life by displaying only good fruit.

What type of a person does adversity cause you to be?

_____
_____
_____
_____
_____
_____
_____
_____
_____
_____
_____
_____
_____
_____
_____
_____
_____
_____
_____
_____
_____
_____
_____
_____

My brethren, count it all joy when you fall into various
trial. (James 1:2 NKJV)

DAY 12

In the Blink of an Eye

It was a sunny Saturday morning when my daughter called me. I could hear how upset she was. Traveling east down a country road on her way to take her puppy to doggy boot camp, she found herself between a rock wall and guard rails, with nowhere to go.

As she was driving, she noticed a utility van slowing veering over into her lane, first with one wheel and then another. The closer she got to it, the more it crossed the yellow line. Before long, all four wheels were coming at her head on. With cars behind her, laying on her horn. She slammed on her brakes and was going off the edge of the road with no other options. In the blink of an eye, the driver corrected the van that had crossed over in front of her. As she relived that moment to me, the pit of my stomach became weak as I played out the image in my mind.

We are not guaranteed tomorrow, today, or even our next breath. How quickly things can change. I am reminded of 1 Corinthians 15:52 NKJV: "In a moment, in the twinkling of an eye, at the last trumpet. For the trumpet will sound, and the dead will be raised incorruptible, and we shall be changed."

Will you be ready when the trumpet sounds? In the blink of an eye, your life could change.

Are you ready?

_____

_____

_____

_____

_____

_____

_____

_____

_____

_____

_____

_____

_____

_____

_____

_____

_____

_____

_____

_____

_____

_____

Behold, I tell you a mystery: we shall not all sleep, but we shall all be changed. (1 Corinthians 15:51 NKJV)

DAY 13

Do It with a Purpose, Not a Checklist

The beginning of a new year brings more resolutions, more goals we plan to accomplish. We all have them. Lose ten, twenty, or more pounds right after the holidays have passed. Exercise daily or form a new habit. Each year, I have set those goals only to fail. I finally realized that it takes more than just a goal to achieve it; it takes a purpose. I finally lost twenty pounds when my A1C was getting close to a critical stage. I knew I had to make a change for my health. I never started to exercise because I knew I wouldn't commit the time to stick with it, but I did have a purpose to change the way I ate and lose the weight.

One goal that I set this year, and many other previous years, was to read the Bible all the way through in a year, which I have failed to do many times. Oh, I have read it through a few times, but I have also failed many more, not necessarily because I quit but because it became a checklist instead of a purpose. I was doing it because I made a vow to do it. I would start out strong, reading every day, then by a few months in, especially when it was a long reading session, I would start falling behind. I would break it up into two or three sessions and before long I would be trying to play catchup by reading as fast as I could but not benefiting from what I had read.

It wasn't until I was in a Bible study that I realized that I was treating my time with God as a box that I checked off. I had gotten away from true worship with my Lord. Before I realized what I was doing, I felt I was struggling to stay near Him, but it wasn't just a feeling. God doesn't care if you read one chapter or a book a day as long as you are in His word, connecting with Him. Step into His space and focus on where He wants you to be instead of where you want to be with your goal. Take the goal or resolution out of the equation. The true act of worship will fulfill your goal a lot faster than a checklist. He deserves so much more than our time. He deserves to be praised and worshipped.

Describe how you study God's word.

_____

_____

_____

_____

_____

_____

_____

_____

_____

_____

_____

_____

_____

_____

_____

_____

_____

_____

_____

_____

_____

_____

_____

_____

Get wisdom! Get understanding! Do not forget, nor turn away from the words of my mouth. (Proverbs 4:5 NKJV)

Take time to write out Psalms 146 through 150 and praise the Lord!

DAY 14

Good Deed 1963

I was on a mission to get a walk-in tub for my parents, without the funds to do so. In three and a half weeks, I was able to put together a benefit dinner and auction with the help of family and friends. Many of my days were spent going from store to store, contacting everyone that my parents had done business with over the past fifty years. The community opened their hearts and their wallets, and we were able to raise almost $13,000 in that time.

I came across many stories and testimonies over those few weeks, but one story was sent from God and blessed my family as well as another. The week before the auction, I advertised in our local paper to promote it and the dinner to get more people to attend. In response to the ad, I received a phone call the day the local paper hit the mailboxes in our county. It was midafternoon when my phone rang; a gentleman was on the other end. We will call him Mr. Jim, and this is how the conversation went.

Me: Hello
Mr. Jim: I just saw an ad in the newspaper.
Me: Yes sir.
Mr. Jim: About a benefit auction.
Me: Yes sir.
Mr. Jim: So, you know what I'm talking about.
Me: Yes sir.
Mr. Jim: Can I tell you a story?
Me: Yes sir (as I smiled).

Mr. Jim: Over sixty years ago, in 1963, I lived on Covington Avenue and I was in the process of moving. My neighbor and his son helped me all day and at the end of the day I asked Marvin Coulter and his son [my grandfather and dad] what I owed them. Marvin told me whatever I could afford, which wasn't much, but I gave them what I could. For the past sixty years, I have thought about that day and it has bothered me all those years that I didn't give them much because I simply didn't have it to give. After reading the ad in the paper about the benefit auction, I realized this was the son of Marvin and I now have the opportunity to pay back a good deed from 1963.

Mr. Jim asked for my address that day because he now had a way to pay back a debt he thought he owed. I told Mr. Jim that he was going to make me cry and of course he said, "That's okay, you just go ahead and cry." He told me that he was always taught that when you do something good it will always come back to you.

What a blessing it was for Mr. Jim to finally be able to return the act of kindness after all these years. We will never know the impact that we can have on someone. The fingerprints of God are all around us and sometimes God allows us to see the good deeds from 1963.

*Make a list of opportunities where you can
pay it forward with good deeds.*

_____

_____

_____

_____

_____

_____

_____

_____

_____

_____

_____

_____

_____

_____

_____

_____

_____

_____

_____

_____

_____

_____

And let us not grow weary while doing good, for in due
season we shall reap if we do not lose heart. Therefore,
as we have opportunity, let us do good to all, especially
to those who are of the household of faith. (Galatians
6:9–10 NKJV)

DAY 15

A Victorious Entry

As I have sat here for several days watching my dad slowly fade away, I am thankful for the time with him the Lord has given me. I wouldn't trade that time for anything.

Dad has always been a big man, standing at six feet four inches and weighing over 200 pounds. He worked hard all his life as a farmer, going strong up until a few weeks before he turned eighty-five. He never gave up or gave in. To see his frail, thin body get weaker and weaker has been hard.

I have prayed that he would not suffer. I am thankful that, for the most part, he has rested comfortably and has only been in pain when he had to be moved or turned over. That has been probably one of the hardest things about taking care of him: knowing I was going to hurt him and all I could do was to say, "I'm sorry."

There have been times that I have broken down and cried at the thought of losing him. There have been times that it has taken all my strength to care for his needs, especially as he has become bedridden. There have been times that I have asked the Lord to forgive me when I have had little patience. I have had times that I have felt that I have not been a very good caregiver but then I think, *God chose me.*

As he is awaiting his victorious entry into Heaven, I have a sense of peace knowing that he is about to meet his Lord and Savior face to face. One day we too will experience that victorious entry if we have Jesus as Lord of our lives and have accepted Him as our Savior.

What will your victorious entry look like?

_____

_____

_____

_____

_____

_____

_____

_____

_____

_____

_____

_____

_____

_____

_____

_____

_____

_____

_____

_____

_____

_____

Then I heard a voice from heaven saying to me, "write: 'Blessed are the dead who die in the Lord from now on.'" "Yes" says the Spirit, "that they may rest from their labors, and their works follow them." (Revelation 14:13 NKJV)

RUTH SMITH

DAY 16

Guardian Angel

On January 16, 1993, I had a normal bedtime routine with my girls and a normal, happy baby. Little did I know that night as I went to bed that I would feel the presence of God. He sent me His guardian angel to wake me during the night. I don't remember if it was a small still voice, a little nudge, or just the awakening. Regardless, I know that He woke me up and sent me directly to the crib of my seven-month-old daughter, who wasn't breathing.

It plays out vividly in my mind to this day. I scooped her up out of the crib and shook her from one end of our mobile home to the other. Finally, she gasped and started breathing again. She then laid her head on me and went back to sleep.

How do I know that there was a guardian angel among us that night? I was awakened and went straight to her crib as if I knew what was wrong. Almost immediately, I was able to lay her back down after she started breathing again. The unusual thing was that I was able to lay down and go to sleep without hesitation, worry, or an unsettled mind.

I am thankful that I had the Lord as my Savior during that time to give me rest and a peace that He would protect us. Psalm 91:11 NKJV tells us "For He shall give His angels charge over you." I don't think I would have had the same peace if I had not known Him as my Savior. It makes me cringe to think that maybe I wouldn't have been awakened to get her out of the crib.

I have a God who is there during my times of need, and I am thankful that He has shown me His fingerprints throughout my life. Today I have a beautiful young lady as my daughter. She has a master's degree in social work and is helping other children get a second chance as I feel God allowed her and me to have.

Are you at peace in your life?

_____

_____

_____

_____

_____

_____

_____

_____

_____

_____

_____

_____

_____

_____

_____

_____

_____

_____

_____

_____

_____

_____

Behold, I send an angel before you to keep you in
the way and to bring you into the place which I have
prepared. (Exodus 23:20 NKJV)

DAY 17

Heaping Coals

An eye for an eye and a tooth for a tooth. For the most part I feel that the world lives by this vengeful way. Why would we let someone get away with doing us wrong? We need to get even. We want them to get what is coming to them, but it needs to be right now, and we want to determine what the punishment will be. That person will pay for what he or she has done if it's the last thing I do.

Does any of this sound familiar? We are commanded to turn the other cheek in Matthew 5:38–44 NKJV, but we think that is impossible. How can we turn the other cheek when a person has wronged us?

Have you ever tried to pay someone back, but it comes back to bite you? Maybe you tried to get even and the one who was in the wrong comes out smelling like a rose. We live in a society that demands justice, but we protest when it goes through a process. All it would take is for us to leave it in God's hands, show ourselves as Christians being Christ like in every way, and He will heap coals of fire upon their heads. Isn't He more able to serve punishment than we are?

God gives us free will, the chance to choose wisely, and the opportunity to love our enemy as He loves. What will you choose to do? 1 Peter 5:7 NKJV tells us to "cast our cares upon Him, for He cares for us." He is telling us to literally throw the problem upon Him and leave it with Him. So many times, we pray about something that worries us or that is stealing our joy. Often times, we pray for the answers we need and then take it right back, not allowing God time to take care of it. When we do this, we are allowing others to steal our joy instead of allowing God to multiply it. Lord, help us to give it to You, that You may cast it into the fire and use the coals as You see fit. God is more powerful than we are to address our problems, so let Him have the shovel.

Whose hand is your shovel in?

_____

_____

_____

_____

_____

_____

_____

_____

_____

_____

_____

_____

_____

_____

_____

_____

_____

_____

Repay no one evil for evil. Have regard for good things in the sight of all men. If it is possible, as much as depends on you, live peaceably with all men. Behold, do not avenge yourselves, but rather give place to wrath; for it is written, "vengeance is Mine, I will repay" says the Lord. Therefore If your enemy is hungry, feed him. If he is thirsty, give him a drink; for in so doing you will heap coals of fire on his head. Do not be overcome by evil but overcome evil with good. (Romans 12:17–21 NKJV)

DAY 18

Michael's Mission

It was early morning on March 15, 2021. The sun was shining, but little did we know that darkness was in the midst. My daughter and son-in-law had been up for a short time when Michael collapsed, leaving my daughter in a state of panic and unbelief. Hard as she tried to bring him back, he was being called home, leaving his wife with their two young sons.

Michael came into our lives in 2006 and married our young daughter of seventeen in 2007 before being deployed to Afghanistan for a year. Needless to say, it was a hard way to start a marriage, but they endured it. In 2019, Michael hit rock bottom as their marriage was falling apart. My heart hurt for Michael and my daughter that year, but I know now that it was a part of God's plan. With a lot of prayer, Michael came to know the Lord on a personal and intimate level and God mended their marriage. If Michael had not hit rock bottom, he may have never come to know Christ on the level that he did.

Michael leaned on Kevin, a former youth pastor and friend, during that time. He dug into God's word seeking to find answers about how to totally surrender his life to Christ. He called Kevin for some work during that time and had started asking harder questions of how to be all in. Kevin illustrated that day by putting his hand in a water trough. As he splashed his hand around a little, he told Michael, "This is where you are, just splashing around." Then Kevin dunked his own head in the water and told him, "This is where you need to be." He pointed Michael to Ephesians chapters 1 through 3 and told him to study it to find his real identity. A short time later, Michael called Kevin and said that he had to talk to him urgently. Michael had to let Kevin know that he finally got it. It wasn't about him; it was only about Christ and living for Christ.

Michael was all in and was on a mission to let everyone know that this is not our home. As Christians, we should all long to go home. We should be sold out, enough that we long to be with the Father as Michael did. As he had told my daughter just four days prior to his death, "I'm ready to go home."

I can see the fingerprints of God that were there from years past. My daughter was on the committee that hired Kevin as the youth pastor who would form a friendship with Michael and lead him to the Lord. Michael's and my daughter's separation led Michael to a deeper relationship with the Lord; it also gave his boys a glimpse of life without their father to make the transition of his death a little more bearable. My youngest daughter became a social worker to help kids. Without a doubt, I know it was to help her nephews deal with the loss of their father and support her sister through this difficult time. But the biggest fingerprint of all was thinking about how young Michael was—only thirty-three. Then it dawned on me, Jesus was thirty-three when He hung on the cross for you and me, and made the biggest impact after His death. Michael's biggest impact for Christ will be after his death.

Those three chapters led Michael to a deeper love for the Lord, his wife, and his boys. I tell this story to honor my son-in-law Michael Bradley Hall, to glorify the Father, and to keep Michael's mission alive.

In memory of my son-in-law Michael who loved my daughter and grandsons so much but loved the Lord more.

Read Ephesians 1-3, discover your identity,
and write it out so you will never forget.

_____
_____
_____
_____
_____
_____
_____
_____
_____
_____
_____
_____
_____
_____
_____
_____
_____
_____
_____
_____
_____
_____
_____

That the God of our Lord Jesus Christ, the Father of
glory may give to you the spirit of wisdom and revelation
in the knowledge of Him. (Ephesians 1:17 NKJV)

DAY 19

911, What's Your Emergency?

For most of us we will never forget 9/11, a day that was terrifying because of the unknown. I remember where I was when the planes crashed into the Twin Towers that day. I can also remember the shambles that my life was in. On January 6 of that year, my husband and I separated, and I could not have cared less. We had grown so far apart, and I was no longer in love with him.

I was raised in church. At the age of eleven, I asked Jesus into my heart and accepted Him as my Lord and Savior. But as I approached my teenage years, I gave into worldly ways: parties, and doing and saying things that were not Christ like. I was not concerned about living for Jesus but doing what I thought was making me "happy".. At the age of eighteen, I married my husband, with whom I was in an ungodly relationship, and had my first child at the age of nineteen. We were playing the role of church goers. We knew our daughter needed to be there so that she would make better choices than we had been making. There were times that we would be on fire for the Lord and then there would be times of backsliding.

After seven or eight years of marriage, the worldly ways were taking over our lives, and we drifted farther and farther apart. In our twelfth year of marriage, I was done. My 911 emergency was my marriage, and I was willing to let it burn to the ground.

As tragic as 9/11 was for so many people, and I would never want to make light of it. We saw story after story of the good that came from it. The event left me scared to be in my home alone with my children. I needed some kind of security blanket, and that would be my husband. We had started living in the same house once again but not as a couple.

Many people were praying for us, and we didn't have a clue that God was working in our lives at the same time. That summer, we went to Florida to chaperone the youth of our church, not knowing that our pastor had other plans for us. We too would be going through the evangelism training, learning to give our testimony, and sharing details of our separation. It wasn't easy, but it was freeing.

More than twenty years have passed since our separation and we have grown in our walk with the Lord and each other. I won't say it has been a bed of roses because we still have our ups and downs. However, it has definitely been a better road to travel since we have had Jesus riding beside us. After thirty-three years of marriage, now I know it takes a lot of work on both sides. Giving up is not an option because we can always add Jesus to the relationship who can make it work.

The fingerprints of God never cease to amaze me when I look back at the years past. I am thankful He is willing to reveal them to me. He is with you, and He can rescue you from the 911 emergency in your life too.

911, what's your emergency?

_____
_____
_____
_____
_____
_____
_____
_____
_____
_____
_____
_____
_____
_____
_____
_____
_____
_____
_____
_____
_____
_____
_____
_____

He is before all things, and in Him all things hold together. (Colossians 1:17 NIV)

DAY 20

God's Perfect Timing

Two years ago, when I started praying for God to give me my heart's desire to stay home and take care of my parents, I thought that it would be within weeks or months not years. At this point in my life, I see that it was not His will for it to have happened when I thought it should have happened. Had I quit my job at that moment, I would have probably just found another job and would not have trusted Him in the process. That, in turn, could have derailed His plans for my life. I may have never been able to leave my job and take care of my parents.

My parents were able to be at home and fairly independent until May of 2020. Even though COVID was a horrible thing for most people, the Lord blessed me through that time. I was able to be at home from March until September that year to help my parents. Then God led me to give my notice and on September 24, 2020, I was able to walk away and take care of my parents full-time.

Mom still has trouble walking and has to use a walker to get around. On February 1, 2021, Dad fell and broke his hip, which led him to have surgery the next day. I know now they will have to have around-the-clock care.

God has been preparing me for this all my life. He has been putting me in different positions within the jobs I have had, and preparing and positioning me for His plan.

Despite the actions that I have taken in my life, God still orchestrated a perfect plan. Again, God knew, positioned me, and allowed me to see His fingerprints just as He did for Joseph in Genesis chapters 37 through 41. God had a plan for Joseph's life, from being sold into slavery by his brothers to being falsely accused and thrown into prison.

God blessed Joseph to interpret dreams. This ultimately led him to be second in command so God could use him to provide for his family through a severe famine. God orchestrated his life to provide; it wasn't always easy, but Joseph opened his heart to follow the path God was leading him down.

Open your eyes and heart to see the evidence that God has been at work in the events of your own life; although it may not have always been easy, give God the glory.

What is God orchestrating in your life for His perfect timing?

_____
_____
_____
_____
_____
_____
_____
_____
_____
_____
_____
_____
_____
_____
_____
_____
_____
_____
_____
_____
_____
_____
_____
_____
_____

"For I know the plans I have for you," declares the Lord,
"plans to prosper you and not to harm you, plans to give
you hope and a future." (Jeremiah 29:11 NIV)

DAY 21

A Thankful Heart

We all have heartache, trials, pain, and sorrow. But how do we respond to those experiences? We are in no way immune to them, and why should we be? Even Mary and Joseph suffered along their journey to Bethlehem. Then there was the suffering that surpassed all suffering when our Lord was ridiculed, spit upon, and beaten so badly that the flesh was ripped from His body. For what? Why would anyone endure that much pain willingly? I am thankful that He loved us that much and was willing.

It was a rough year, from losing a young son-in-law in March to losing my dad in September. We have had our share of heartache, pain, and sorrow but I can still have a thankful heart. I am thankful that my daughter's marriage of thirteen years had gotten better the last six months that her husband was here on earth. I am thankful that my grandson was able to shoot his hunting rifle with his dad for the first time the day before Michael passed away. I am thankful for the time I got to spend with my dad before the Lord called him home. I am thankful for all the memories I have of him, for the peace of knowing where my dad is, and knowing he is not going through the pain we must endure here on earth. No matter what you are going through or facing, remember that you are not alone. We can still have thanksgiving in our hearts.

In times of trials, pain and sorrow what are you thankful for?

Giving thanks always for all things to God the Father in the name of our Lord Jesus Christ. (Ephesians 5:20 NKJV)

DAY 22

Ouch! That's My Toes
You're Stepping On!

God uses the Holy Spirit to convict us. As Christians, we feel it. Have you ever sat in church and just couldn't be comfortable or became weak to your stomach? I sure have—too many times to count. As Christians we often refer to this as getting our toes stepped on.

You may feel that the preacher is looking right at you, like he knows exactly where you have fallen short. However, I guarantee it has nothing to do with what the preacher is thinking and everything to do with the words God is speaking through him. He is convicting you while stepping on your toes.

"If your toes are being stepped on, you may need to walk in a different direction" is one of my favorite church sign sayings. God allows us to choose the wrong paths. I mean, after all, we are human. Don't get me wrong—I know it doesn't feel good. However, that pain is a wonderful tool the Holy Spirit uses to draw us back to Him. There, we can grow and become better followers and examples of Christ. That painful path could alter the direction your life is going in, so choose to see it as God blessing you.

Remember, while conviction doesn't feel very good it does remind us that we need to repent. We may have to take the long way home at times, but thankfully Jesus is there with the lights on, ready to open the door of forgiveness.

What direction are you walking? Is it
the path that God has for you?

_____

In all of your ways acknowledge Him, and He shall
direct your paths. (Proverbs 3:6 NKJV)

DAY 23

A Samaritan's Heart

The Samaritan journeyed and came across a man who had been beaten, broken, and left for dead. He had compassion on him without counting the cost. He was only concerned about caring for his needs. This reminds me of my cousin who also doesn't count the cost.

In June of 2015, my cousin was admitted to the hospital after several years of sickness. As her health rapidly declined and infection spread throughout her body, she shared with her family that she thought the Lord was calling her home.

The family was called in and told that nothing else could be done, but God had other plans. The family doctor, seeing her family's great faith, was not about to give up on God either. All the doctors and nurses said it was a miracle from God when she went home a month later, and we know that it truly was.

She had a long road ahead of her, to say the least. In 2016, her body could no longer absorb and retain the nutrients and electrolytes that she needed to survive. Now, she spends four days a week, and an average of eight hours each of those days, getting infusions, and she is on a continuous feeding tube.

She has daily battles with her health, probably the most I have ever seen in one person. She does not let that stop her from praying for those who are sick and suffering, calling to check on the shut-ins, even making a three-hour drive just to be near family for their comfort, all while her labs were in critical range.

One of her favorite life verses is Philippians 4:19 NKJV—"My God shall supply all your needs according to His riches in Christ Jesus"—and she lives it as such. She once told me that she has learned "there is power and peace in prayer and there are blessings received in the midst through others that are used as the hands and feet of Jesus."

She deals with her own personal pain of nausea and vomiting. Sometimes, she is too weak to even walk, but she pushes through that she may bless those around her. She makes a daily difference in the lives of others, whether by encouraging or bringing hope and inspiration to others as they face their own difficult journeys. Even when she is weak, she shows so much strength. A Samaritan's heart never counts the cost.

What can you do today to show a Samaritan's heart?

_____

_____

_____

_____

_____

_____

_____

_____

_____

_____

_____

_____

_____

_____

_____

_____

_____

_____

_____

_____

"But a certain Samaritan as he journeyed, came where he was. And when he saw him, he had compassion." (Luke 10:33 NJKV)

DAY 24

The Beauty of the Redwoods

I really never had the chance to travel until the last few years and I think it's in my blood now. Every three or four months, I am ready to go and do something, somewhere. I eagerly wait for the next time I get to hop in the car or on a plane, even if it's just to get away for a few days. I investigate places that I see advertised to determine if I would like to visit them. I listen for things that may pique my interest.

A few months ago, I heard someone describing the Redwood Forest as resilient and strong. I listened as they explained why they have the characteristics that they have. Redwoods have shallow roots that can run up to as much as 100 feet just beneath the earth's surface. They intertwine with the roots of other redwoods, giving them the strength and stability to be strong together. Otherwise, they could not stand when the storms come upon them. They were created to be resilient and resistant to insects, fungi, and fire, giving them the remarkable ability to survive all that comes their way.

Much like the redwoods, God has created us to be resilient to the worldly ways of this life. The Bible helps us to resist those who persecute us, the fall that temptations bring, and the destruction that Satan tries to bring to our lives and churches. There is strength in numbers. As the redwoods need other redwoods to stand strong, we too need one another as Christians to stand strong. When Satan tries to create havoc in our lives, remember the beauty of the redwoods standing strong and resilient.

How do you stand strong in the Lord?

_____

_____

_____

_____

_____

_____

_____

_____

_____

_____

_____

_____

_____

_____

_____

_____

_____

_____

_____

_____

Two are better than one, because they have a good reward for their labor. For if they fall, one will lift up his companion. But woe to him who is alone when he falls, for he has no one to help him up. (Ecclesiastes 4:9–10 NKJV)

RUTH SMITH

Write out Romans 8:1-39

_____

_____

_____

_____

_____

_____

_____

_____

_____

_____

_____

_____

_____

_____

_____

_____

_____

_____

_____

_____

_____

_____

_____

_____

_____

_____

_____

_____

_____

DAY 25

Give Thanks

How many times a day do you pray? The Bible tells us to pray continually. When you pray, does your mind wander and become distracted by the world around you? Maybe you pray only for yourself, with no thought for others, and forget to praise God with a sincere and thankful heart for what He has done. God is more concerned with the sincerity of our thanks and praise than our words.

Prayer is meant to be a private and personal conversation with the Father. It is an intimate talk, not one of repetition and idle words. He loves for you to pour your heart out to Him. It is a time not only for petition but a time to give thanks. Psalm 92 NKJV tells us, "It is good to give thanks to the Lord."

Many times, we (including myself) get in a habit with our prayers and never say a prayer from our hearts. We thank Him for our food, for the day, and for all that He does, with no feeling behind the words. Our prayer life becomes stagnant—it is just mere words. Don't get me wrong—we do need to take time to thank Him for those things. However, I think the psalmist is telling us to give thanks of worship in song, dance, and praise—in other words, to worship Him with *all* our hearts.

Sometimes I think when we pray, we forget that it takes a heart connection to communicate with God. In turn, we miss and fail to see the fingerprints and the blessings that He leaves on our hearts and lives.

Today, take thirty minutes out of your day to have a little talk with Jesus and truly worship the Lord with thanksgiving. This could be taking a quiet moment with inspirational music, lifting your voice with your hands held high, or dancing before the Lord as if no one were watching—as if it was just you and Him. I know, you're thinking that is silly. However, God didn't think David was silly when he danced before the Lord in 2 Samuel 6:1–22 NKJV and stated, "I am willing to look foolish." You know David had a smile on his face and joy in his heart as He worshiped his Lord. For Jesus, real worship comes from the heart.

How will you give thanks today?

_____
_____
_____
_____
_____
_____
_____
_____
_____
_____
_____
_____
_____
_____
_____
_____
_____
_____
_____
_____
_____
_____
_____

Let them praise His name with the dance; let them
sing praises to Him with the timbrel and harp. (Psalm
149:3 NKJV)

DAY 26

A New Day

Opportunity after opportunity—each day we have an opportunity to share, to learn, to trust, and to love. How do we use the opportunities that we are given? I'm not going to lie; I stumble and even struggle with this at times.

I have let the opportunity of sharing Christ pass me by, when I knew that He was leading me to do so, only to feel guilt and shame after the fact. I knew I would never have that same opportunity again, or that it was at that very moment that their hearts were ready to receive.

I am thankful the Lord gives us new days with new opportunities to make a difference in the lives of others. This could be by smiling, showing others God's love, or taking the opportunity to share the gospel that could possibly lead them to salvation.

On two distinct occasions over the last year, I remember not following where God was leading and missing the opportunities He had put before me. I am learning that it is okay to feel fear but it's not to act on fearful feelings. That's exactly what I did on one of those occasions. I was at a family resource office when a young man came in and inquired about job openings in the area. He was told that they could not help him, even though there were job postings everywhere. He was told that he would have to go to the unemployment office a county away. I thought how sad it was that they wouldn't give him the time of day. But what I saw and didn't respond to next was the saddest of all.

When I left the building, the young man was sitting in the truck beside me with a young woman and what looked to be a baby just a few weeks old in her arms. I sat in my car thinking, to myself, *Go over and see if there is something you can do. Have prayer, offer to buy milk and baby formula, or to share the opportunity of being self-employed, as I am. Most of all share the love of Jesus with them.* Fear set in, even though I know that feeling fear is simply the temptation to run away from what we should confront. As I backed out of my parking spot and drove away, I was overcome with guilt and shame because I knew I would never have that same opportunity with that couple again. What if that was their only chance to meet Jesus?

Months later, I let my busyness get in the way of reaching an individual who had allowed the world to consume him. I had the opportunity to visit him, but I let time get away from me. I thought I would do it the next day, and then it was too late. He had moved, and I had no way to find him. The only thing I could do then was to pray that the time he spent in solitude was enough time to recommit his life to Christ. My heart was burdened for him to come back to Christ. I had the opportunity to put that thought back in his heart and I missed it.

Even though I can't go back and change those situations, I can rest assured that God makes all things new again. He gives me new opportunities to reach others and allows me to see the fingerprints where I messed up so that I can learn from them.

Lord, strengthen and guide me in every opportunity You give me that You may be glorified.

What will you do with this new day God has given you?

_____

_____

_____

_____

_____

_____

_____

_____

_____

_____

_____

_____

_____

_____

_____

_____

_____

_____

_____

_____

Do not remember the former things, nor consider the things of old. (Isaiah 43:18 NKJV)

DAY 27

And Time Stood Still

I have lived on the same farm on a one-lane road since I was two. I remember as a kid walking to our neighbors' house across the creek, a little less than two tenths of a mile away. I can remember walking slowly, not in a hurry for anything.

Our neighbors were in their late fifties, but as a kid I felt as if they were in their nineties. It's funny how we perceive things as a child. I can remember sitting on their porch, listening as they told stories. I can remember Sunday afternoons spent with family during the summer months, outside in the yard, running around and playing, because it meant something. It was as if time stood still.

Today's society moves at such a fast pace; we are always in a rush to get from this baseball game to that soccer practice or whatever takes us from here to there. We cram as much into our days as we can—so much that we forget to take time for the most important parts of our lives.

Distractions are all around us, making it easy to slip away from church or to lose track of our prayer lives and Bible study. We are all guilty. If I allow my daily routine to get messed up or something happens to throw off my morning, then my spiritual life suffers.

When we have a hard time being still, we should pray that God gives us stillness—stillness to rest our minds and souls. Make a list of the things that distract you and pray that God helps you overcome them. I'm not saying it will be easy. I struggle most days to get up early, and I allow my tiredness to get in the way so that I don't have life's distractions. Remember this: even Jesus had to find ways to get away from the crowds so He could be still. May time stand still for you today while you spend time with the Lord.

What will you do with the time the Lord has given you?

Be still and know that I am God. (Psalm 46:10 NKJV)

DAY 28

A Lasting Legacy

What would you consider to be your greatest accomplishment in life? What kind of a lasting legacy do you see yourself leaving? No matter what we do, how much we gain, or how much we have, it will never compare to the lasting legacy that we have when we experience salvation.

How does salvation become a lasting legacy? It happens by sharing our faith, testimony, and the life of salvation through our Lord Jesus Christ. We leave legacies that continue to reach others. We may never see the end results and that's okay; if we do, that is just icing on the cake. Either way, we can know that God used us and His fingerprints will leave a lasting legacy on generations to come.

In Matthew 28, we are commanded to go. In Ezekiel, He speaks of not warning the lost. God will accomplish His work through you or through someone else. We can choose to be obedient and allow Him to use us while blessing us. We can also choose not to be a part of the task He has orchestrated for us. He will accomplish the task through someone else, while we miss out on the blessings He had in store for us.

Why would we keep it to ourselves? We are held accountable for not sharing the gospel. We are guilty, and we stop a legacy when we choose not to share. We can choose to live lives of obedience where we follow, do His will for our lives, and be blessed by His presence. We do not save—that is the Lord's job—but we can lead, or we can hinder. We are all called to leave lasting legacies.

What kind of legacy will you leave?

_____

_____

_____

_____

_____

_____

_____

_____

_____

_____

_____

_____

_____

_____

_____

_____

_____

_____

_____

_____

_____

Nevertheless, if you warn the righteous man that the righteous should not sin, and he does not sin, he shall surely live because he shall surely live because he took warning; also you will have delivered your soul. (Ezekiel 3:21 NKJV)

DAY 29

Days of Doubt

No matter how strong our walks with the Lord are, periods of doubt have happened to us all at some points and times in our lives. How many times have you said, "I doubt that" or "I doubt that will ever happen"?

I think that we should all have Thomas or Peter in our names. Thomas and Peter were disciples, the ones closest to Jesus, walking along side of Him and seeing the miracles that He performed first hand. They still had doubts.

In Mathew 14:26–31 NKJV, Peter, in his unbelief, thought he was seeing a ghost as Jesus walked on the sea. Peter asked for proof as he asked the Lord to allow himself to walk on water as well. Peter climbed out of the boat and began to walk on water but started to sink as soon as he took his eyes off Jesus and began to doubt. Most of us remember the story of doubting Thomas. Thomas was with Jesus daily and heard His teachings that warned him and the other disciples of what was to come. Thomas had doubts and disbeliefs that Jesus had appeared to the disciples behind closed doors, as recorded in John 20:24–29 NKJV. He stated that He would only believe if could see the print of the nails in His hands or put his hand in His side.

I had doubts about writing this devotional book and finishing it, not to mention getting it published. Why? Because I am not a writer and I thought there is no way "I" can do this. I was right: I couldn't do it and I didn't stop to think about the fact that it wasn't me doing it in the first place. Actually, I was doubting God, not myself.

At the end of the day, Peter and Thomas were human and experienced the same lack of faith that we experience. Lord help us in our unbelief.

Where do you need to ask God to help you in your unbelief?

_____

_____

_____

_____

_____

_____

_____

_____

_____

_____

_____

_____

_____

_____

_____

_____

_____

_____

_____

_____

_____

_____

And immediately Jesus stretched out His hand and caught him, and said to him, "O you of little faith, why did you doubt?" (Matthew 14:31 NKJV)

DAY 30

Room at the Table

I love to sit on my porch and watch the hummingbirds. If you watch long enough, they are quite comical. I have three different feeders with at least four feeding ports each. However, they always tend to go to the same feeder, and they all want that feeder as their own. They don't want to share in the sweetness of the nectar. They will swoop down at one another and chase each other around. They remind me of fighter jets after the enemy.

As I was watching them go back and forth one evening, I was reminded that there is room at the table and that the Kingdom of God is like a banquet with plenty for all. We don't have to fight for a seat or wonder if there will be enough. All we must do is accept the invitation.

In Luke 14:15–24 (NKJV) we are taught the parable of "The Great Supper." Many were invited, but some let the priorities of the world get in the way and declined the invitation. The master told the servant to go out into the streets and bring in the poor and the lowly. After doing so, the servant told his master there was still room. The master told the servant to compel them to come, that his house may be filled.

God calls us to go and compel the lost to come to Him. Verse 24 tells us that the ones who chose not to come would not taste His supper. You are invited and there is room at His table for you.

*Have you accepted the invitation? If so, what
can you do to compel others to come?*

"Then the master said to the servant, 'Go out into the highways and hedges, and compel them to come in, that my house may be filled. For I say to you that none of those men who were invited shall taste my supper.'" (Luke 14:23–24 NKJV)

THE PLAN OF SALVATION

If you have not accepted Jesus as your Lord and Savior, know that God has a plan and purpose for your life. He loves you and wants to come into your heart. The cross is the only bridge to fill the gap. Here is how you can receive Christ as Lord of your life. It's as easy as A, B, C.

First, admit that you are a sinner. Be willing to repent and turn away from your sins.

> For all have sinned and fall short of the Glory of God. (Romans 3:23 NKJV)

Second, believe that Jesus Christ died for your sins.

> But God demonstrates His own love toward us, in that while we were still sinners, Christ died for us. (Romans 5:8 NKJV)

Third, confess that Jesus is Lord.

> If you confess with your mouth the Lord Jesus and believe in your heart that God has raised Him from the dead, you shall be saved. (Romans 10:9 NKJV)

If you are ready, please pray this prayer with me.

> Lord, I know that I am a sinner and I want to become the person you want to be. I believe that you died on the cross for me and rose from the grave. I ask that you forgive me of my sins and that you would be Lord of my life, Amen.

Thank you to all who supported this book

Gold Sponsors

Smith Contracting LLC

Parkview IGA

Linda Toupin National Sales Dir. Emeritus

Kim Noel

John McDaniel

Travis and Julie Tackett

Kelly Conley

Hall's Shepherds

Catherine Stewart

Carey and Son Funeral Home

Hickory Hill Garden Center and Florist, Inc.

Edward and Claudia Fisher

Darlene Ferguson

Handy Andy's Handy Man Services

Amy L. Turpin

Short Construction

Katie Toupin

Parkview Home Center

Stan and Cheryl Coulter

Jeff Coulter

Medley's Towing Service

Diane McDaniel

Tammy Godbey

Jamie Smith

Nally Tire and Automotive

Diane Anderson

Rakes Drywall LLC

Silver Sponsors

Small Town Curbing LLC

Giggles and Grins Boutique LLC

Sale With Hale

Mary Piatt

Virginia Coulter

Tracy Galloway

NOTES

NOTES

NOTES

NOTES

NOTES

Printed in the United States
by Baker & Taylor Publisher Services